GW01191333

THE DOOR OF MERCY

in the words and life of Pope Francis

by
Fr Ivano Millico

*All booklets are published thanks to the
generous support of the members of the
Catholic Truth Society*

CATHOLIC TRUTH SOCIETY
PUBLISHERS TO THE HOLY SEE

Contents

All rights reserved. First published 2015 by The Incorporated Catholic Truth Society, 40-46 Harleyford Road London SE11 5AY Tel: 020 7640 0042 Fax: 020 7640 0046. © 2015 The Incorporated Catholic Truth Society.

ISBN 978 1 78469 079 3

THREE WORDS OF INTRODUCTION

The Door

What is a door for? And what is a *Door of Mercy* for? Every day we pass through many doors: house doors and front gates; car and train doors.

But passing through a door is not just going in and out.
A door pierces a wall and opens a new space.
A door is there not just to make me 'pass-through' but to make me 'pass-over', to allow me to experience a change.

Throughout history God has been opening doors:

the door of Noah's ark, to save mankind from the waters of the flood (cf *Gn* 6:16);

the doorposts of the houses of the Israelites, to free them from slavery (cf *Ex* 12:22);

the door of the Temple in Jerusalem, to enter into the glory of God (cf *Ez* 43:4);

the prison door of Peter's cell, to deliver him from death (cf *Ac* 12:1-11).

All these many doors point to one door,
Christ, who said, "*I am the door*" (*Jn* 10:9).

This one door was opened wide on the cross, when Christ opened his hands and his body was pierced by a lance (cf *Jn* 19:34).

Finally, there is the door of the tomb where the body of Christ lay. In vain did the soldiers place a large stone against it (cf *Mk* 16:4).

"Let us go across to the other side"

On that day, when evening had come, Jesus said to them, 'Let us go across to the other side.' And leaving the crowd they took him with them in the boat. (*Mk* 4:35-36)

These are the words of Christ to us as we are about to enter the *Door of Mercy*.

The '*other side*' is the side of Mercy, where, by receiving mercy, we become merciful.

The call to '*go across*' is the urgent need for our conversion.

'*That day*' is to last a whole year, as an extraordinary moment of grace, a Holy Year.

The '*boat*', made of timber, is like a bridge, a door, the Good News, our hope.

This small booklet is a sort of boat-crossing manual!
It is meant to help us to '*cross to the other side*', especially those of us who are a bit lost, in the dark or tired, as '*evening had come*'.

Finally, before beginning our journey, we hear that
'*they took him with them in the boat*'.
The crossing is not made on our own, but with a companion, someone who has done the journey before and who knows 'the way of mercy'.[1]
Our boat companion is Pope Francis, his life and his words.

The 'doorkeeper'

Standing in front of any door, we look for a bell, a handle, an opening…
But this door, the *Door of Mercy*, is already open.

"*As I looked, there before me, I saw a door standing open in heaven*". (*Rv* 4:1)
Yet in the first book of the Bible we read that the door to heaven had been walled off (cf *Gn* 3:23). The sin of man closed the door. The mercy of God reopened the door.

The *Holy Year of Mercy* is our journey from sin to mercy, through an opened door!

But who has opened the door?

In the ancient Church a person was charged with a particular service, called the 'ministry of the ostiary' or 'of the door'. Every Christian community had a doorkeeper, someone who would receive the brothers and sisters, open the door to them, and lead them in.

Our 'doorkeeper' is Pope Francis, with his words and his life.

Pope Francis will be our guide through this *Holy Year of Mercy*, showing us the way, opening the door for us, and leading us to meet mercy.

"As I looked, there before me, I saw a door standing open in heaven...And I heard a voice as of a trumpet speaking to me, saying: 'Come'". (*Rv* 4:1)

Come, said the doorkeeper.

Let us begin "our year-long journey with an open heart to receive the mercy of God."[2]

One of the Pharisees asked Jesus to eat with him, and he went into the Pharisee's house and took his place at the table. And a woman in the city, who was a sinner, having learned that he was eating in the Pharisee's house, brought an alabaster jar of ointment. She stood behind him at his feet, weeping, and began to bathe his feet with her tears and to dry them with her hair. Then she continued kissing his feet and anointing them with the ointment.

Now when the Pharisee who had invited him saw it, he said to himself, "If this man were a prophet, he would have known who and what kind of woman this is who is touching him - that she is a sinner."

Jesus spoke up and said to him, "Simon, I have something to say to you." "Teacher," he replied, "Speak."

"A certain creditor had two debtors; one owed five hundred denarii, and the other fifty. When they could not pay, he cancelled the debts for both of them. Now which of them will love him more?"

Simon answered, "I suppose the one for whom he cancelled the greater debt."

And Jesus said to him, "You have judged rightly."

Then turning toward the woman, he said to Simon, "Do you see this woman? I entered your house; you gave me no water for my feet, but she has bathed my feet with her tears and dried them with her hair. You gave me no kiss, but from the time I came in she has not stopped kissing my feet. You did not anoint my head with oil, but she has anointed my feet with ointment. Therefore, I tell you, her sins, which are many, are forgiven; hence she has shown great love. But the one to whom little is forgiven, loves little."

Then he said to her, "Your sins are forgiven." But those who were at the table with him began to say among themselves, "Who is this who even forgives sins?"

And he said to the woman, "Your faith has saved you; go in peace."

(*Lk* 7:36-50)

WHAT IS MERCY?

In this booklet you will read the word 'mercy' repeated over and over again.

But what is it? What is 'mercy'?

Our God, the God of Abraham, the God of Isaac, the God of Jacob, the God of Israel, the Father of our Lord Jesus Christ, is a merciful God, a God rich in mercy.

But 'mercy' is not so much a quality of God, a divine attribute.

The word 'mercy' speaks not simply of God on his own, but of God in relationship with his people, especially the weak, the poor and the sinners.

In this sense, more than a noun, 'mercy' is a verb, an action; it is the action of God who turns towards those who are suffering, who runs towards those who are in sin, who hears the cry of the poor, who responds to the oppression of his people, who embraces all our poverties including our greatest poverty - death - and raises us up giving us new life. "It is a force which gives life, which raises a dead man. God's mercy gives life to man, it raises him from the dead."[3]

God is love, and "mercy" is a particular way in which God loves us.

"It is the attitude of God in contact with human misery, with our destitution, our suffering, our anguish. The biblical term 'mercy' (compassion) recalls a mother's womb. The mother in fact reacts in a way all her own in confronting the pain of her children. It is in this way, according to Scripture, that God loves us.[4]

Mercy is not a feeling, an emotion, or a biblical concept.

Mercy is God who comes to meet my sufferings, touch my sins, heal my misery.

It is an answer. The answer of God to evil, our lack of life, our sin and death.

Every time you come across the word 'mercy', it says first of all something about you, and then something about how God loves you.

WE ARE PILGRIMS

ear pilgrim,

The *Holy Year of Mercy* is a journey.
This makes of us a pilgrim.

This small booklet is for your pilgrim's bag.
Its purpose is to accompany you to the threshold
of the *Door of Mercy*,
to help you not simply to go in and out,
but to go across to the other side,
to experience a 'passover':
to receive mercy so to become merciful.

Every chapter of this booklet, every image, every
Gospel passage, is a like a step forward along the
'way of mercy';
sometimes a big step, other times a pause.
Take your time.

A pilgrim does not run, but walks…

ONE JOURNEY, TWO PEOPLE

Pope Francis announces the Holy Year of Mercy

The *Holy Year of Mercy* begins on the Solemnity of the Immaculate Conception, 8th December 2015, and comes to a close on 20th November 2016, the Solemnity of Our Lord Jesus Christ King of the Universe.

The *Holy Year of Mercy* is more than a calendar event; it is a journey, and more than a journey. It is the experience of a change of direction. It is the basic experience "of the Christian life… the 'exodus' experience… an experience of Passover… the journey of each Christian soul and the entire Church, the decisive turning of our lives".[5]

Announcing the Extraordinary Jubilee of Mercy at a Lenten penitential celebration in Saint Peter's Basilica, Pope Francis spoke of one journey and two people travelling the 'way of mercy' (cf *Lk* 7:36-50): one who walked the whole way and encountered mercy; the other who stopped at the threshold and could not find the way to mercy.

The sinful woman and the Pharisee

One journey, two people. The sinful woman found her way to Jesus through her sins: "she opened her heart; in sorrow, she showed repentance for her sins; by her tears, she appealed to divine goodness to receive forgiveness.

For her there will be no judgement but that which comes from God, and this is the judgement of mercy."[6] But for the master of the house, Simon the Pharisee, "everything is calculated, everything is thought out...he stands firm on the threshold of formality. He is not capable of taking that next step forward to meet Jesus who will bring him salvation. Simon limits himself to inviting Jesus to lunch, but did not truly welcome him."[7]

The guest - Jesus, the mercy of God - is in his very house, but Simon the Pharisee does not meet him. The sinful woman, instead, while standing outside, is drawn into the house, crosses the door of mercy with tears of repentance, and meets Jesus. She touches mercy, she is touched by mercy, and she herself becomes merciful.

One journey, two people!
If you are 'the sinful woman', this booklet is for you: remember your own journey, where you come from, and how much you have been loved.

If you are 'the Pharisee', this booklet is for you: do not to stop at the threshold of your pride but, attracted by the guest in the house, return to yourself. Do not be afraid to move, because the guest is already running towards you, and "do not forget that God forgives all, and God forgives always."[8]

Whoever you are, "mercy will always be greater than any sin"[9] you have committed or will commit.

"This is Me, a Sinner on whom the Lord has Turned His Merciful Gaze"

Pope Francis in his own words

Pope Francis knows the journey to mercy.

He has told us so.

In August 2013, Pope Francis met several times with Father Antonio Spadaro SJ, editor-in-chief of the Jesuit magazine *La Civiltà Cattolica*. The text of Pope Francis's first interview came out in September and created widespread interest. Reflecting on this experience, Fr Spadaro decided to publish the full text of his one-to-one conversation with the pope, enriched by 'behind-the-scenes' anecdotes from when his voice-recorder was switched off.

Fr Spadaro recalls how as he sat in front of the pope, following an initial friendly exchange somehow he decided not to follow the script he had prepared, and instead asked off-the-cuff: "Who is Jorge Mario Bergoglio?"

The Pope stares at me in silence… and says to me: "I do not know what might be the most fitting description…I am a sinner. This is the most accurate definition. It is not a figure of speech, a literary genre.

I am a sinner…Yes, but the best summary, the one that comes more from the inside and I feel most true is this: I am a sinner whom the Lord has looked upon."[10]

A sinner whom the Lord has looked upon with mercy

This is Pope Francis in his own words! Insisting that this is not just a figure of speech but a profound self-understanding, the Pope made reference to an image dear to him, *The calling of St Matthew* as painted by Caravaggio. Fr Spadaro recalled how, as if changing topic, the Pope continued:

"I do not know Rome well…I know St Mary Major, St Peter's…but when I had to come to Rome, I always stayed in [the neighbourhood of] Via della Scrofa. From there I often visited the Church of St Louis of France, and I went there to contemplate the painting *The Calling of St Matthew* (cf *Mt* 9:9-13) by Caravaggio.

"That finger of Jesus, pointing at Matthew. That's me. I feel like him. Like Matthew. It is the gesture of Matthew that strikes me: he holds on to his money as if to say, 'No, not me! No, this money is mine.' Here, this is me, a sinner on whom the Lord has turned his gaze. And this is what I said when they asked me if I would accept my election as pontiff."

Then the Pope whispered in Latin: "I am a sinner, but I trust in the infinite mercy and patience of our Lord Jesus Christ, and I accept in a spirit of penance."[11]

MISERANDO ATQUE ELIGENDO

The Motto of Pope Francis

When Jorge Mario Bergoglio was chosen as auxiliary bishop of Buenos Aires in 1992 he chose as his episcopal motto the Latin words *Miserando atque Eligendo*, which come from a homily by Bede the Venerable on the Feast of Matthew: *Vidit ergo Jesus publicanum, et quia miserando atque eligendo vidit, ait illi*, "*Sequere me*".

"Jesus therefore sees the tax collector, and since he sees by having mercy and by choosing, says to him, 'Follow me'."

Elected pope, Francis decided to keep his existing coat of arms:

[The motto *Miserando atque Eligendo*] has particular significance in the life and spirituality of the Pope. In fact, on the Feast of St Matthew in 1953, the young Jorge Bergoglio experienced, at the age of seventeen, in a very special way, the loving presence of God in his life. Following confession, he felt his heart touched and he sensed the descent of the Mercy of God, who with a gaze of tender love, called him to religious life, following the example of St Ignatius of Loyola.[12]

By having mercy and by choosing him

Commenting on Bede's words in his conversation with Fr Spadaro, the pope said:

> "I am one who is looked upon by the Lord. I always felt my motto, *Miserando atque Eligendo* [by having mercy and by choosing him], was very true for me."

And in a style proper to him, the pope coined a new word:

> "I think the Latin gerund *miserando* is impossible to translate in both Italian and Spanish. I like to translate it with another gerund that does not exist: *misericordiando*, 'mercy-ing'."[13]

The mercy of God for Matthew the tax-collector, the mercy of God for Jorge Mario Bergoglio, the sinner, the mercy of God for me and you is "not an abstract idea", but a concrete action, "God's action from the very beginning of the history of mankind after the sin of Adam and Eve".[14]

> As Jesus was walking along, he saw a man called Matthew sitting at the tax office; and he said to him, "Follow me." And he got up and followed him.
>
> And as he sat at dinner in the house, many tax collectors and sinners came and sat down with Jesus and his disciples. When the Pharisees saw this, they

said to his disciples, "Why does your teacher eat with tax collectors and sinners?" But when he heard this, he said, "Those who are well have no need of a physician, but those who are sick. Go and learn what this means, 'I desire mercy, not sacrifice.' For I have come to call not the righteous, but sinners."

(*Mt* 9:9-13)

"It Changed My Life"

Pope Francis's encounter with mercy

When you hear Pope Francis speaking of 'mercy' you get a distinct feeling that he is speaking first-hand, from a direct experience. For Pope Francis, 'mercy' is not so much a quality of God, a biblical concept, but a fact, an event, a meeting, an encounter: the encounter between a sinner, a repentant sinner, and God. In his words, "not an abstract idea of mercy, but rather a concrete experience".[15]

This is Pope Francis's experience of mercy, as told us by himself. On the 21st September 1953, the feast of St Matthew, the young Jorge Mario Bergoglio, not yet seventeen, was preparing to celebrate 'Students' Day' at the beginning of springtime (in the southern hemisphere) with an outing. But beforehand, not really knowing why, he went to his local parish church, the church of San José de Flores, where he saw a priest he had never met before who transmitted to him a great sense of spirituality. He felt moved to go to confession. There something happened.

Recalling those moments, he said:

Something strange happened to me in that confession. I don't know what it was, but it changed my life. I think it surprised me, caught me with my guard down. It was the surprise, the astonishment of a chance encounter. I realized that they were waiting for me.[16]

Remembering that confession before being ordained priest in 1969, Bergoglio wrote down his 'confession of faith': "I believe in my history, which was moved by God's loving gaze on that spring day, 21st September, when he came to greet me and invite me to follow him."[17]

The gaze of Jesus

Fifty years later, by now Archbishop and Cardinal, Bergoglio had been invited to the International Book Fair in Buenos Aires to present the latest book by Luigi Giussani, the Italian founder of the movement Communion and Liberation. Presenting the book - *L'attrattiva Gesù* ['The Attraction of Jesus'] - Bergoglio went back to that 'initial experience' of the gaze of Jesus turned towards him. He said:

Everything in our life begins with an encounter. An encounter with this Man, the carpenter of Nazareth, a man like all men and yet different. The first ones, John, Andrew, and Simon, felt themselves to be looked at into their very depths, read in their innermost being, and in them sprang forth a surprise, a wonder that instantly made them feel bound to him, made them feel different.[18]

Our response, our answer to this initial gaze, our conversion, is not the fruit of efforts or good will. No. Our response to Christ - our Christian life - is part of that very same encounter, it is generated by that encounter, it is the 'grace', we can say, of that very encounter.

The tenderness of mercy

Bergoglio continued with surprising words:

We cannot understand this dynamic of encounter which brings forth wonder and adherence if it has not been triggered - forgive me the use of this word - by mercy. Only someone who has encountered mercy, who has been caressed by the tenderness of mercy, is happy and comfortable with the Lord. I beg the theologians who are present not to turn me in to the Sant'Uffizio or to the Inquisition; however, forcing things a bit, I dare to say that the privileged locus of the encounter is the caress of the mercy of Jesus Christ on my sin. In front of this merciful embrace we feel a real desire to respond, to change, to correspond; a new morality arises. We posit the ethical problem, an ethics which is born of the encounter, of this encounter which we have described up to now. Christian morality is not a titanic effort of the will, the effort of someone who decides to be consistent and succeeds, a solitary challenge in the face of the world. No. Christian morality is simply a response. It is the heartfelt response to a surprising, unforeseeable, 'unjust' mercy. The surprising, unforeseeable, 'unjust' mercy, using purely human criteria, of one who knows me, knows my betrayals and loves me just the same, appreciates me, embraces me, calls me again, hopes in me, and expects from me. This is why the Christian conception of morality is a revolution; it is not a never falling down but an always getting up again. As we shall see, this authentic, in a Christian sense, conception of morality which Giussani presents has nothing to do with the spiritualistic-type quietisms of which the shelves of the religious supermarkets of today are full. Trickery. Nor with the Pelagianism so fashionable today in its different, sophisticated manifestations. Pelagianism, underneath it all, is a remake of the Tower of Babel. The spiritualistic quietisms are efforts at prayer and immanent spirituality which never go beyond themselves.[19]

We need to be loved in our sins

It is necessary to meet mercy; it is necessary for my conversion, for my life as a Christian. We need to be forgiven, we need to be looked upon with mercy, we need to be known as we are, we need be loved in our sins. And the encounter with this 'unjust' mercy, a mercy which I do not deserve and I cannot attain, happens in the Church.

The *Door of Mercy* is the door of our community, of our local church, of the Church, which opens to us "the space where Christian life matures, by enabling one to experience the mercy of God."[20]

"The Most Powerful Gospel: the Gospel of Mercy"

The first homily of Pope Francis

Pope Francis was elected pope on 13th March 2013. It was a Wednesday, Wednesday of the fourth week of Lent. The following Sunday, his first Sunday as pope, he celebrated Mass in the parish church of St Anne inside the Vatican walls.

After the gospel reading - the adulterous woman (cf *Jn* 8:1-11) - Pope Francis said:

> [T]his is the message of the Church for today, that of [God's] mercy towards this woman…the message of Jesus for us: mercy. I think - and I say it with humility - that this is the Lord's most powerful message: mercy. It was he himself who said: "I did not come for the righteous… I came for sinners" (*Mk* 2:17).

And to anyone who dares saying "Oh, I am a great sinner!", Pope Francis announced:

> "Neither do I condemn you; go, and sin no more" (*Jn* 8:11). He [Jesus] comes for us, when we recognise that we are sinners. But if we are like the Pharisee, before the altar, who said: I thank you Lord, that I am not like other men, and especially not like the one

at the door, like that publican (cf *Lk* 18:11-12), then we do not know the Lord's heart, and we will never have the joy of experiencing this mercy! Let us ask for this grace.[21]

The scribes and the Pharisees brought a woman who had been caught in adultery and making her stand before all of them, they said to him,

"Teacher, this woman was caught in the very act of committing adultery. Now in the law Moses commanded us to stone such women. What do you say about her?"

They said this to test him, so that they might have some charge to bring against him. Jesus bent down and wrote with his finger on the ground. When they kept on questioning him, he stood up and said to them, "Let him who is without sin among you be the first to throw a stone at her." And once more he bent down and wrote with his finger on the ground. But when they heard it, they went away, one by one, beginning with the eldest; and Jesus was left alone with the woman standing before him. Jesus looked up and said to her, "Woman, where are they? Has no one condemned you?"

She said, "No one, sir." And Jesus said, "Neither do I condemn you. Go, and do not sin again."

(*Jn* 8:3-11)

"MERCY CHANGES EVERYTHING"

The first Angelus of Pope Francis

After greeting parishioners outside the church, the pope went to Saint Peter's Square for his first Angelus: "Mercy changes everything, it changes the world".

Commenting again the episode of the adulterous woman, he said:

Brothers and Sisters, God's face is the face of a merciful father who is always patient. Have you thought about God's patience, the patience he has with each one of us? That is his mercy. He always has patience, patience with us, he understands us, he waits for us, he does not tire of forgiving us if we are able to return to him with a contrite heart. 'Great is God's mercy'.[22]

"This is the Time of Mercy"

from the Second Vatican Council to Pope Francis

During a press conference on his return flight from the World Youth Day in Rio de Janeiro, Pope Francis said:

I believe that this is the season of mercy…And I believe that this is a *kairos*: this time is a *kairos* of mercy. John Paul II had the first intuition of this, when he began with Faustina Kowalska, the Divine Mercy… He had something, he had intuited that this was a need in our time.[23]

Again, opening his Lenten meditation with the parish priests of Rome, he said:

Our time is the time of mercy, for the whole Church. I am sure of this. We are living in a time of mercy… This was an intuition of Blessed John Paul II. He 'sensed' that this was the time of mercy…It is up to us, as ministers of the Church, to keep this message alive, above all through preaching and in our actions, in signs and in pastoral choices.[24]

The announcement of an extraordinary Jubilee of Mercy and its coincidence with the anniversary of the closing of the Second Vatican Council - 8th December 2015 and 1965 - has not come as a surprise to many.

In his opening address at the Second Vatican Council, St John XXIII said:

> At this present time, the Church, bride of Christ, prefers to make use of the medicine of mercy... by means of this Ecumenical Council the Church desires to show herself to be the loving mother of all, benign, patient, full of mercy.[25]

Blessed Paul VI spoke about the 'medicine of mercy' in his Encyclical Letter *Ecclesiam Suam* as the necessary mission of the Church:

> A physician who realises the danger of disease, protects himself and others from it, but at the same time strives to cure those who have contracted it, likewise the Church does not regard God's mercy as an exclusive privilege...showing more concern and more love for those who live close at hand or to whom it can go in its endeavour to make all alike share the blessing of salvation.[26]

One Sunday afternoon, after the Angelus, Pope Francis surprised everyone in St Peter's square when he pulled out from his pocket a little white box called *Misericordina* 'the medicine of mercy'! Francis the 'pharmacist' said: "Do not forget to take it, because it is good for you. It is good for the heart, the soul, and for life in general!"[27]

Some of us need to take this medicine once a day, some twice a day, some even more often...and there are no side effects.

Then Jesus said, "There was a man who had two sons. The younger of them said to his father, 'Father, give me the share of the property that will belong to me.' So he divided his property between them. A few days later the younger son gathered all he had and travelled to a distant country, and there he squandered his property in dissolute living.

"When he had spent everything, a severe famine took place throughout that country, and he began to be in need. So he went and hired himself out to one of the citizens of that country, who sent him to his fields to feed the pigs. He would gladly have filled himself with the pods that the pigs were eating; and no one gave him anything. But when he came to himself he said, 'How many of my father's hired servants have bread enough and to spare, but here I am dying of hunger! I will get up and go to my father, and I will say to him, "Father, I have sinned against heaven and before you; I am no longer worthy to be called your son; treat me like one of your hired servants." '

"So he set off and went to his father. But while he was still far off, his father saw him and was filled with compassion; he ran and embraced him and kissed him. Then the son said to him, 'Father, I have sinned against heaven and before you; I am no longer worthy to be called

your son.' But the father said to his slaves, 'Quickly,
bring out a robe - the best one - and put it on him; put
a ring on his finger and shoes on his feet. And bring the
fatted calf and kill it, and let us eat and celebrate; for
this son of mine was dead and is alive again; he was lost
and is found!' And they began to celebrate.

(*Lk* 15:11-24)

"The Merciful Father"

Pope Francis's favourite gospel

If you were to ask Pope Francis about his favourite Gospel passage, he will most definitively answer the parable of 'the Merciful Father' or, as we know it, "the Prodigal Son' (cf *Lk* 15:11-32). Referring to the 'three parables of mercy' we read in Chapter Fifteen of the Gospel of Luke, Pope Francis exclaimed: "Here is the entire Gospel! Here! The whole Gospel, all of Christianity, is here!"[28] "I am always struck," confessed the Pope, "when I reread the parable of the merciful Father; it impresses me because it always gives me great hope."[29]

A rebellious son who turns his face and his life away from God, who finds himself in sin, in despair, in a trap, in a pit of death and loneliness. A son moved to return. A Father who keeps silent, who loves his son as he is, who allows him to sin, to go away, to do his own will.

Where can they meet again? Where can they be reconciled? Where can the Father forgive his son, where can the son experience the mercy of the Father?

How can a lost son return?

Stepping out of the door

The parable speaks of the house of the Father (cf *Lk* 15:25), a house with a door, the door through which the son walked out, going away. How did the father react? Did he close the door behind, as his son left? Did he change the lock, in case the son decided to come back? Did he bolt the door to teach his son a lesson? No. In his very first General Audience, Pope Francis - and I am not aware of any one before him speaking in these terms - tells us what the father did once his son had left the house. The merciful father also stepped out from the door! He went looking, searching for his son in the distance every single day. He did not remain inside, closed in the house waiting on his sofa for his son to return. No:

> He went every day to see if his son was coming home: this is our merciful Father...he was waiting for him with longing on the terrace of his house. God always thinks mercifully. He is the merciful Father! God thinks like the father waiting for the son and goes to meet him, he spots him coming when he is still far off.[30]

We are the son of the parable, and the *Door of Mercy* is the door of the house of God the Father, the door to a life of communion with God and with the other brother of the story. And "God's patience has to call forth in us the courage to return to him, however many mistakes and

38

sins there may be in our life."[31] The meeting with mercy,
the embrace between the merciful Father and the repentant
son, does not happen inside the house, and not even at the
doorsteps. The meeting happens outside the house, because
the Father is already outside his door: "God has come out
of himself" in Jesus Christ in order to meet us where we
are. There, where we are, there he is coming to love us and
forgive us. "God does not wait for us to go to him but it
is he who moves towards us, without calculation, without
quantification. That is what God is like. He always takes
the first step, he comes towards us."[32]

The Patient Father

And again:

Jesus is all mercy, Jesus is all love: he is God made
man. Each of us, each one of us, is that little lost
lamb, the coin that was mislaid; each one of us is
that son who has squandered his freedom on false
idols, illusions of happiness, and has lost everything
(cf *Lk* 15). But God does not forget us, the Father
never abandons us. He is a patient father, always
waiting for us! He respects our freedom, but he
remains faithful forever. And when we come back
to him, he welcomes us like children into his house,
for he never ceases, not for one instant, to wait for
us with love. And his heart rejoices over every child
who returns. He is celebrating because he is joy. God

has this joy, when one of us sinners goes to him and asks his forgiveness.[33]

Think of that younger son who was in the Father's house, who was loved; and yet he wants his part of the inheritance; he goes off, spends everything, hits rock bottom, where he could not be more distant from the Father, yet when he is at his lowest, he misses the warmth of the Father's house and he goes back. And the Father? Had he forgotten the son? No, never. He is there, he sees the son from afar, he was waiting for him every hour of every day, the son was always in his father's heart, even though he had left him, even though he had squandered his whole inheritance, his freedom. The Father, with patience, love, hope and mercy, had never for a second stopped thinking about him, and as soon as he sees him still far off, he runs out to meet him and embraces him with tenderness, the tenderness of God, without a word of reproach: he has returned! And that is the joy of the Father. In that embrace for his son is all this joy: he has returned! God is always waiting for us, he never grows tired. Jesus shows us this merciful patience of God so that we can regain confidence, hope - always! It is like a dialogue between our weakness and the patience of God, it is a dialogue that, if we do it, will grant us hope.[34]

"Doors of Mercy"

Our Christian experience

During the *Holy Year of Mercy* doors are to be opened, *doors of mercy*.

First of all, the Holy Door of St Peter's Basilica, then the Holy Doors of the other three major papal basilicas in Rome. Then follows the holy door of every diocesan cathedral, and the doors of our local churches.

But what does it mean to walk through a *Door of Mercy*? What is it like?

Is it like an airport security door scanning all my sins and sending out alarm sounds?

Is it a magical door that somehow has the power to cleanse me as I walk through?

Are they religious revolving doors that spin me around, so that in the end I find myself back where I started only more disorientated?

Or, perhaps, can something new happen to me during this *Holy Year of Mercy*?

The Threshold of Faith

The *Door of Mercy* are 'holy', said Pope Francis, because they open to us a way forward, a "path of conversion".[35] The opening of the *Door of Mercy* is nothing else but a 'new exodus', the opening of the Red Sea (cf *Ex* 14), a new path that God himself opens for us, to 'pass-over' from old ways to a new life, to be set free from slavery to sin and enter into a Promised Land, to taste new fruits and experience God's unconditional love for us sinners. Pope Francis comments:

> The image of the door recurs in the Gospel on various occasions and calls to mind the door of the house, of the home, where we find safety, love and warmth. Jesus tells us that there is a door which gives us access to God's family, to the warmth of God's house, of communion with him. This door is Jesus himself (cf *Jn* 10:9). He is the door. He is the entrance to salvation. He leads us to the Father and the door that is Jesus is never closed. This door is never closed it is always open and to all, without distinction, without exclusion, without privileges. Because, you know, Jesus does not exclude anyone. Some of you, perhaps, might say to me: "But, Father, I am certainly excluded because I am a great sinner: I have done terrible things, I have done lots of them in my life". No, you are not excluded! Precisely for this reason you are the

favourite, because Jesus prefers sinners, always, in order to forgive them, to love them. Jesus is waiting for you to embrace you, to pardon you. Do not be afraid: he is waiting for you. Take heart, have the courage to enter through his door. Everyone is invited to cross the threshold of this door, to cross the threshold of faith, to enter into his life and to make him enter our life, so that he may transform it, renew it and give it full and enduring joy.[36]

The Discovery of God

The experience of the *Holy Year* is nothing but our basic Christian experience, the paschal dynamic, our passing from a way of living centred on myself, where everything turns round my ego, "with all its variations: me, with me, for me, only me, always egoism, I!"[37], to a way of living where I am 'de-centred' and my life is lived for others. This is a decisive turning of our lives away from ourselves and towards God and the other: "an ongoing exodus out of the closed inward-looking self towards its liberation through self-giving, and thus towards authentic self-discovery and indeed the discovery of God".[38]

The *Holy Year of Mercy* is not just another religious initiative, another box to tick. "Let us not fall into humiliating indifference or a monotonous routine that prevents us from discovering what is new! Let us ward off destructive cynicism!"[39]

The *Holy Year* makes present an experience, a dynamic movement.

In fact, crossing the *Door of Mercy* makes present two movements. First, a 'going out' - a movement outside of myself;[40] then a 'going forward' - a movement towards others, especially those most in need. This Passover, this 'exodus' is the faith journey of each Christian and of the entire Church. What is 'extraordinary' during this *Holy Year of Mercy* is the grace of this time when we can truly move forward, genuinely convert and experience a real change in our life.

Strike out on the path

Speaking of this 'exodus' in his message for the World Day of Prayer for Vocations, Pope Francis wrote:

Christian life is...a constantly renewed attitude of conversion and transformation, an incessant moving forward, a passage from death to life like that celebrated in every liturgy, an experience of Passover. From the call of Abraham to that of Moses, from Israel's pilgrim journey through the desert to the conversion preached by the prophets, up to the missionary journey of Jesus which culminates in his death and resurrection, vocation is always a work of God. He leads us beyond our initial situation, frees us from every enslavement, breaks down our habits and our indifference, and brings us to the joy of communion with him and with our brothers and sisters. Responding to God's call, then, means allowing him to help us leave ourselves and our false security behind, and to strike out on the path which leads to Jesus Christ, the origin and destiny of our life and our happiness.[41]

The Church, "a House of Mercy"

The mission of the Church

What is the name of your church?
The name of your parish?

Pope Francis has coined a new term: 'House of Mercy'. "How greatly I desire," Pope Francis exclaimed, "that all those places where the Church is present, especially our parishes and our communities, may become islands of mercy in the midst of the sea of indifference!"[42]

The image of a house makes immediately think of four closed walls. Speaking of the holy house of Loreto, and of the Church as a house, Pope Benedict XVI said something very beautiful:

Its location on a street is well known. At first this might seem strange: after all, a house and a street appear mutually exclusive. In reality, it is precisely here that an unusual message about this House has been preserved. It is not a private house, nor does it belong to a single person or a single family, rather it is an abode open to everyone placed, as it were, on our street.[43]

The Church is a house and a street at the same time

A house of mercy is always both 'indoors' and 'outdoors' because of the *Door of Mercy*: a house where wounds can be healed with the oil of mercy, and a street into which we can go out to announce the mercy of God.

The Church "is Jesus's house and Jesus welcomes, but not only does he welcome: he goes to find people". "And if the people are wounded," the Pope asked, "what does Jesus do? Does he rebuke them for being wounded? No, he comes and carries them on his shoulders." This, the Pope said, "is called mercy".[44]

And again:

> No one can be excluded from the mercy of God; everyone knows the way to access it and the Church is the house where everyone is welcomed and no one is rejected. Her doors remain wide open, so that those who are touched by grace may find the assurance of forgiveness. The greater the sin, the greater the love that must be shown by the Church to those who repent. With how much love Jesus looks at us! With how much love he heals our sinful heart![45]

The Church is a mother

The Church is a mother: she has to go out to heal those who are hurting, with mercy. If the Lord never tires of forgiving, we have no other choice than this: first of all, to care for those who are hurting. The

Church is a mother, and she must travel this path of mercy. And find a form of mercy for all. When the prodigal son returned home, I don't think his father told him: "You, sit down and listen: what did you do with the money?" No! He celebrated! Then, perhaps, when the son was ready to speak, he spoke. The Church has to do this, when there is someone…not only wait for them, but go out and find them! That is what mercy is.[46]

At the first of his Wednesday catecheses on the Church, Pope Francis said how the 'building' of the Church as a 'House of Mercy' does not rest in our initiative but in God.

The love of God precedes everything. God is always first, he arrives before us, he precedes us. The Prophet Isaiah, or Jeremiah, I don't remember, said that God is like an almond blossom, because it is the first tree to flower in spring. Meaning that God always flowers before us. When we arrive he is waiting for us, he calls us, he makes us walk. Always anticipating us. And this is called love, because God always waits for us. God is waiting for you. And if you were a great sinner he is waiting for you even more and waiting for you with great love, because he is first. This is the beauty of the Church, who leads us to this God who is waiting for us! He precedes Abraham, he precedes even Adam.[47]

The Balm of God's Mercy

In his very first homily before the new Cardinals, Pope Francis said:

> The Church's way, from the time of the Council of Jerusalem, has always, always been the way of Jesus, the way of mercy and reinstatement. This does not mean underestimating the dangers of letting wolves into the fold, but welcoming the repentant prodigal son; healing the wounds of sin with courage and determination; rolling up our sleeves and not standing by and watching passively the suffering of the world. The way of the Church is not to condemn anyone for eternity; to pour out the balm of God's mercy on all those who ask for it with a sincere heart. The way of the Church is precisely to leave her four walls behind and to go out in search of those who are distant, those essentially on the 'outskirts' of life. It is to adopt fully God's own approach, to follow the Master who said: "Those who are well have no need of the physician, but those who are sick; I have come to call, not the righteous but sinners".[48]

Another image which speaks of the Church as a house which is at the same time 'indoors' and 'outdoors' is the image of the heart. Pope Francis has called mercy "the beating heart of the Gospel".[49] And our heart has two movements, two beats, in and out, receiving mercy and dispensing mercy.

What about my heart? Do I suffer from a condition hardening the heart?

"This is the opportune moment to change our lives! This is the time to allow our hearts to be touched! Opening our hearts to the hope of being loved forever despite our sinfulness."[50]

"THE WHIP OF MERCY"

The beginning of the journey,
our spiritual conversion

In his announcement of the Jubilee Year, Pope Francis said: this *Holy Year of Mercy* is a journey, a "journey which begins with *spiritual conversion*".[51] *Spiritual conversion*: these words echo the very same words used by Blessed Pope Paul VI as he officially announced his Extraordinary Jubilee Year on the 7th December 1965, at the vigil of the closing of the Second Vatican Council.[52] Fifty years later, the grace and the call of this Jubilee Year is the same: "a singular opportunity of spiritual conversion".[53]

Mercy is a 'journey', a journey of conversion, "and we," said Pope Francis, "have to make this journey".[54]

Every journey has a beginning, a starting point. What is then the first step of the journey of conversion leading to receive mercy and so to become merciful?

During the week leading to the announcement of the *Holy Year of Mercy*, Pope Francis, during his daily mediations at the Mass in the chapel of the *Domus Sanctae Marthae*, spoke at length, and in surprising terms, about this 'journey of conversion'.

Blaming Oneself

The first step on our path of conversion is to look at ourselves, to feel ashamed because of our sins, to accuse rather than justify ourselves and pointing the finger at the faults of others, and to ask for mercy and forgiveness. This is the first step on the path of conversion which leads us to the gift of mercy. Therefore, Pope Francis said, "if we do not learn this first step of life, we will never make progress on the path of Christian life, of spiritual life". This is because "the first step" is "blaming oneself"! Commenting on the daily reading from the Book of Daniel, where the People of God publicly beat their breast and say 'we have sinned' (cf *Dn* 9:4-10), Pope Francis underlined how the people "ask for forgiveness, but not a forgiveness with words: this request for forgiveness is for a forgiveness that comes from the heart because the people feel they are sinners". The people "do not feel they are sinners in theory - because all of us can say 'we are all sinners', it's true, it's the truth: everyone here! - but before the Lord they tell of the bad things they have done and the good things they have not done".

Going further, the Pope recognised how "we all have an alibi" to justify "our sins". What's more, the Pope added, we often put on a face: "I don't know!" or "I didn't do it, it must have been someone else!". In other words, we are always ready to 'play innocent' The Pope warned, however, that, like this, "we don't go forward in the Christian life". Thus, he reiterated, the capacity for self-blame is "the first step", a step we take every day, during the day, and before we end our day.

Indeed, "when we begin to look at what we are capable of, we feel bad, we feel disgust", and we ask ourselves: "Am I capable of doing this?" For example, "when I find envy in my heart and I know this envy is capable of speaking ill of another and morally killing him", I have to ask myself: "Am I capable of it? Yes, I am capable!" This is precisely "how this knowledge begins, this wisdom to blame oneself".

The Roots of Sin that are in us

To illustrate, the Pope gave a practical example. In a simple way, he spoke extraordinary words. When we pass by a prison, he said, we might think that the inmates "deserve it". But, he asked:

> Do you know that were it not for the grace of God, you would be there? Have you thought that you too are capable of doing the things that they did, even worse? [This] is to blame ourselves, not to hide from ourselves the roots of sin that are in us, the many things we are capable of doing, even if they aren't visible.

This attitude, Francis continued, "leads us to feel shame before God". Hence, in our daily dialogue with the Lord we can say: "Look, Lord, I am disgusted with myself, but you are great: to me belongs shame, to you - and I ask for it - mercy".

There is a dynamic of mercy whereby "when one learns to blame himself he is merciful with others". And he is able to say: "Who am I to judge him, if I am capable of doing worse things?" Instead, "how we like to judge others, to speak ill of them!" It is certainly not an easy road, the one which "begins with blaming oneself, it begins from that shame before God and from asking forgiveness from him: ask forgiveness". It is precisely "from that first step we arrive at what the Lord asks us: to be merciful".[55]

The Path of Conversion

The following morning, Pope Francis continued his reflection on the 'path of conversion' and warned us against the pretence of appearing "better than we really are" and so putting ourselves outside the need of for conversion. How often do we say to ourselves, I am already converted!

I don't do evil; I go to Mass every Sunday, I am a good Christian, I make many offerings. We are all very clever [as sinners], say the right things, but do the opposite. [These] clever ones [are] hypocrites [because they] pretend to convert, but their heart is false: they are liars…their heart does not belong to the Lord; it belongs to the father of all lies, Satan. And this is the 'pretence' of holiness.

Francis would ask them: "Have you gone into your heart? Are you able to blame yourself for the things you find there?" Along the path of conversion we need to watch out for "the 'trap', of 'making a pretence' of converting and taking the path of hypocrisy". Jesus, said Pope Francis, preferred sinners "a thousand times" over hypocrites, because at least "sinners told the truth about themselves". The path of conversion is a path of truth not of hypocrisy: "If you take this path, the one to which I invite you, even if your sins are like scarlet, they will become as white as snow".[56]

The Whip of Mercy

The following Sunday at the Angelus, commenting on the Gospel of the expulsion of the merchants from the temple (cf *Jn* 2:13-25), Pope Francis spoke of the "whip of mercy".

He said:

Do we allow him [Jesus] to 'cleanse' our hearts and to drive out the idols, those attitudes of cupidity, jealousy, worldliness, envy, hatred, those habits of gossiping and tearing down others. Do I allow him to cleanse all the behaviours that are against God, against our neighbour, and against ourselves? Each one can answer for him/herself, in the silence of his/ her heart: "Do I allow Jesus to make my heart a little cleaner?" "Father, I fear the rod!" But Jesus never

strikes…Jesus cleanses with tenderness, mercy, love.
Mercy is his way of cleansing. Let us, each of us, let
us allow the Lord to enter with his mercy - not with
the whip, no, with his mercy - to cleanse our hearts.
The whip of Jesus with us is his mercy. Let us open
to him the door so that he will make some cleansing
in us.[57]

"The Sacrament of Mercy"

We are all sinners, going to confession

The day before the announcement of the *Holy Year of Mercy* Pope Francis addressed the participants of a training course on the Sacrament of Reconciliation, and said: "Among the Sacraments, certainly Reconciliation renders present with particular efficacy the merciful face of God". In fact, the mercy of God "is constantly and ceaselessly made real and manifest through this sacrament."[58]

The *Holy Year of Mercy* is a time of grace when we "look at your sins, at our own sins: we are all sinners, all of us. This is the starting point".[59] We need to go to confession!

But how shall I approach the confessional box? How can I go to confession, perhaps after many years, and maybe having had a bad experience?

Going to confession is a "meeting with Jesus who is waiting for us, as we are". And "when the Lord forgives us, he does justice. First of all, he does justice to himself, because he came to save and when he forgives us he does justice to his very self."[60]

Often in his meditations Pope Francis has warned us not to think of confession as going to the dry cleaners who remove the stain of our sins, so that we can go out feeling pure and perfect. Nor it is to enter a torture chamber, and be interrogated, accused, or even beaten up. Now, "in confession, it's true, there's a judgement, because the priest judges", saying: "you've done harm here, you did". However, the Pope explained, "it is more than a judgement: it's an encounter, an encounter with the good God who always forgives, who forgives all, who knows how to celebrate when he forgives, and who forgets your sins when he forgives you." Not something "mechanical", "a practice, a formality", but "the encounter with the Lord who reconciles, embraces you and celebrates".[61]

This is how God forgives: always

But "how does God forgive?" Pope Francis asked himself.

First of all, God always forgives! He never tires of forgiving. It is we who tire of asking forgiveness. But he never tires of forgiving…when Peter asks Jesus: how often shall I forgive, seven times? [he was told,] not seven times, but seventy times seven (cf *Mt* 18:21-22). [In other words,] always, [because] this is how God forgives: always…if you have lived a life of many sins, many bad things, but at the end, contritely ask for forgiveness, he forgives you straight away. He always forgives.

Not only does God "always forgive", but he also forgives "all: there is no sin that he would not forgive". Perhaps, the Pope explained, someone could say: "I don't go to confession because I have done so many bad things, so many of those things for which I will not be forgiven". However "it isn't true", Pope Francis emphasised, because "if you go contritely", then God "forgives all". And "many times he doesn't let you speak: you start asking for forgiveness and he makes you feel that joy of forgiveness before you have finished saying everything". It is just "as it happened with that son who, after squandering all the money of his inheritance with an immoral life"; then "he repented" and prepared a speech to present to his father. However, "when he arrived the father didn't let him speak, he embraced him: because he forgives all. He embraced him".

And more: "there is another thing God does when he forgives: he celebrates". And this "is not imagined, Jesus says it: 'There will be a feast in heaven when a sinner goes to the Father'". Truly, "God celebrates". Thus, "when we feel our heart heavy with sins, we can say: let's go to the Lord to give him joy, so that he may forgive us and celebrate". God works in this way: "He always celebrates because he reconciles".

God "forgets"

There is "something beautiful about the way God forgives: God forgets". Hence, God forgets, and "if one of us goes to the Lord" and says, "do you remember, in that year I did something bad?", he answers, "no, no, no. I don't remember", because "once he forgives he no longer remembers, he forgets…so often, with others, we 'keep a record': this one did this, another one once did that". But God doesn't do this: "he forgives and forgets". So Francis asks himself, "if he forgets, who am I to remember the sins of others?" The Father "forgets, always forgives, forgives all, celebrates when he forgives, and he forgets, because he wants to reconcile, he wants to encounter us".

It is an encounter of healing, the encounter between a sick man and woman and the physician. In his series of Wednesday audiences on the sacraments, Pope Francis said:

> The Sacrament of Reconciliation is a sacrament of healing. When I go to confession, it is in order to be healed, to heal my soul, to heal my heart and to be healed of some wrongdoing. The biblical icon which best expresses them in their deep bond is the episode of the forgiving and healing of the paralytic, where the Lord Jesus is revealed at the same time as the physician of souls and of bodies.[62]

The Younger Son

In front of a confessional box, we may feel utterly discouraged.

Commenting on the parable of the prodigal son, Pope Francis recognises that when we are faced with our sins, our little faith, our poverty, we can be tempted to say to ourselves:

> My sin is so great, I am as far from God as the younger son in the parable…I don't have the courage to go

back, to believe that God can welcome me and that he is waiting for me, of all people. But God is indeed waiting for you; he asks of you only the courage to go to him… For God, we are not numbers, we are important, indeed we are the most important thing to him; even if we are sinners, we are what is closest to his heart…Adam, after his sin, experiences shame, he feels naked, he senses the weight of what he has done; and yet God does not abandon him: if that moment of sin marks the beginning of his exile from God, there is already a promise of return, a possibility of return. God immediately asks: "Adam, where are you?" He seeks him out. Jesus took on our nakedness, he took upon himself the shame of Adam, the nakedness of his sin, in order to wash away our sin: by his wounds we have been healed. Remember what Saint Paul says: "What shall I boast of, if not my weakness, my poverty?" Precisely in feeling my sinfulness, in looking at my sins, I can see and encounter God's mercy, his love, and go to him to receive forgiveness.[63]

Be courageous and go to Confession!

"I would like to ask you [and it is not me asking, but Pope Francis] - but don't say it aloud, everyone respond in his heart: when was the last time you made your confession? Everyone think about it…

Two days, two weeks, two years, twenty years, forty years?

Everyone count, everyone say "when was the last time I went to confession?"

And if much time has passed, do not lose another day. Go, the priest will be good.

Jesus is there, and Jesus is more benevolent than priests, Jesus receives you, he receives you with so much love. Be courageous and go to confession!"[64]

> "Now his elder son was in the field; and when he came and approached the house, he heard music and dancing. He called one of the slaves and asked what was going on. He replied, 'Your brother has come, and your father has killed the fatted calf, because he has got him back safe and sound.' Then he became angry and refused to go in. His father came out and began to plead with him. But he answered his father, 'Listen! For all these years I have been working like a slave for you, and I have never disobeyed your command; yet you have never given me even a young goat so that I might celebrate with my friends. But when this son of yours came back, who has devoured your property with prostitutes, you killed the fatted calf for him!'
>
> "Then the father said to him, 'Son, you are always with me, and all that is mine is yours. But we had to celebrate and rejoice, because this brother of yours was dead and has come to life; he was lost and has been found.'"
>
> (Lk 15:24-32)

"Yes, Mercy...
but Make Sure..."

*Before passing through the Door,
a word of warning from Pope Francis*

In the Gospel the essential thing is mercy. God sent his Son, God made himself man in order to save us, that is, in order to grant us his mercy.[65]

As we stand in front of the *Door of Mercy*, in front of the wounds of mercy, in front of the house of mercy wide open to us, in front of our Merciful Father, in front of the parables of mercy and of the Gospel of Mercy…in front of the *Holy Year of Mercy* for us, Pope Francis warns us of a big danger, the trap into which the other son of the Father fell, the one who believes he is 'righteous' or 'saintly':

But make sure that it is not sentiment, it is not being a 'do-gooder'! On the contrary, mercy is the true force that can save man and the world from the 'cancer' that is sin, moral evil, spiritual evil. Only love fills the void, the negative chasms that evil opens in hearts and in history. Only love can do this, and this is God's joy!

What is the danger? It is that we presume we are righteous and judge others. We also judge God, because we think that he should punish sinners, condemn them to death, instead of forgiving. So, yes, then we risk staying outside the Father's house! Like the older brother in the parable, who rather than being content that his brother has returned, grows angry with the father who welcomes him and celebrates. If in our heart there is no mercy, no joy of forgiveness, we are not in communion with God, even if we observe all of his precepts, for it is love that saves, not the practice of precepts alone. It is love of God and neighbour that brings fulfilment to all the Commandments. And this is the love of God, his joy: forgiveness. He waits for us always! Maybe someone has some heaviness in his heart: "But, I did this, I did that..." He expects you! He is your father: he waits for you always!

Be Merciful

If we live according to the law "an eye for an eye, a tooth for a tooth", we will never escape from the spiral of evil. The evil one is clever, and deludes us into thinking that with our human justice we can save ourselves and save the world! In reality, only the justice of God can save us! And the justice of God is revealed in the Cross: the Cross is the judgement of God on us all and on this world. But how does God judge us? By giving his life for us! Here is the supreme act of justice that defeated the prince of this world once and for all; and this supreme act of justice is the supreme act of mercy. Jesus calls us all to follow this path: "Be merciful, even as your Father is merciful" (*Lk* 6:36)".[66]

"WOUNDS OF MERCY"

Christ, the Door of Mercy

Here I am, standing at the *Door of Mercy*!
I have arrived, but suddenly I have become afraid; I have lost the sense of this journey, as if the doors of the house were shut.

Then, dear pilgrim, remember the words of Jesus to the hesitant Thomas: "put your finger here…put out your hand, and place it in my side" (cf *Jn* 20:27).

We too can enter into the wounds of Jesus, we can enter through the wounds of mercy.

Jesus invites us to behold these wounds, to touch them as Thomas did, to heal our lack of belief. Above all, he invites us to enter into the mystery of these wounds, which is the mystery of his merciful love.

Through these wounds, as in a light-filled opening, we can see the entire mystery of Christ and of God: his Passion, his earthly life - filled with compassion for the weak and the sick - his incarnation in the womb of Mary. And we can retrace the whole history of salvation: the prophecies - especially about the Servant of the Lord, the Psalms, the Law and the Covenant; to the liberation from Egypt, to the first

Passover and to the blood of the slaughtered lambs; and again from the Patriarchs to Abraham, and then all the way back to Abel, whose blood cried out from the earth. All of this we can see in the wounds of Jesus, crucified and risen; with Mary, in her Magnificat, we can perceive that "his mercy extends from generation to generation" (cf *Lk* 1:50)"[67]

Grace abounds

Quoting a homily of St Bernard, Pope Francis said:

"Through the wounds of Jesus I can suck honey from the rock and oil from the flinty rock (cf *Dt* 32:13), I can taste and see the goodness of the Lord" (*On the Song of Songs*, 61:4). It is there, in the wounds of Jesus, that we are truly secure; there we encounter the boundless love of his heart. Thomas understood this. St Bernard goes on to ask: But what can I count on? My own merits? No, "My merit is God's mercy. I am by no means lacking merits as long as he is rich in mercy. If the mercies of the Lord are manifold, I too will abound in merits" (*ibid.*, 5). This is important: the courage to trust in Jesus's mercy, to trust in his patience, to seek refuge always in the wounds of his love. St Bernard even states: "So what if my conscience gnaws at me for my many sins? 'Where sin has abounded, there grace has abounded all the more' (*Rm* 5:20)" (ibid.)"[68]

Quoting once more from one of St Bernard commentaries on the Song of Songs on the mystery of the Lord's wounds, he says that "through these wounds the secret of [Christ's] heart is laid opened to us, the great mystery of love is made manifest, the entrails of mercy of our God are open".[69]

Dear pilgrims, who are to cross the *Door of Mercy*: "behold the way," exclaimed Pope Francis, "which God has opened for us finally to go out from our slavery to sin and death, and thus enter into the land of life and peace. Jesus, crucified and risen, is the way and especially his wounds full of mercy."[70]

MARY, MOTHER OF MERCY

Mercy, *misericordia* as far as I know, is a feminine noun in most languages.

The face of mercy is first of all a female face, the face of a woman, a mother.

Let us turn to Mary, Mother of Mercy.

Salve Regina

Mater misericordiae

Vita, dulcedo, et spes nostra, salve.

Ad te clamamus exsules filii Hevae.

Ad te suspiramus, gementes et flentes

in hac lacrimarum valle.

Eia ergo, Advocata nostra,

illos tuos misericordes oculos ad nos converte.

Et Iesum, benedictum fructum ventris tui,

nobis post hoc exsilium ostende.

O clemens, o pia, o dulcis

Virgo Maria

Hail, holy Queen,

Mother of mercy,

hail, our life, our sweetness and our hope.

To thee do we cry, poor banished children of Eve.

To thee to we send up our sighs, mourning and weeping

in this vale of tears.

Turn, then, most gracious advocate,

thine eyes of mercy toward us,

and after this, our exile,

show unto us the blessed fruit of thy womb, Jesus.

O clement, O loving, O sweet

Virgin Mary.

Endnotes

[1] Pope Francis, *Misericordiae Vultus, Bull of Indiction of the Extraordinary Jubilee of Mercy*, §3.

[2] Pope Francis, *Homily*, Celebration of Penance, 13th March 2015.

[3] Pope Francis, Angelus, 9th June 2013.

[4] *Ibidem.*

[5] Pope Francis, *Message for the 52nd World Day of Prayer for Vocations*, 26th April 2015.

[6] Pope Francis, *Homily*, Celebration of Penance, 13th March 2015.

[7] *Ibidem.*

[8] Pope Francis, *Misericordiae Vultus*, Bull of Indiction of the Extraordinary Jubilee of Mercy, §3.

[9] *Ibidem.*

[10] Pope Francis with Antonio Spadaro, *My Door is Always Open, A Conversation on Faith, Hope and the Church in a Time of Change*, Bloomsbury, 2014, p. 17.

[11] *Ibidem*, pp.18 and 19.

[12] The description of the Coat of Arms of Pope Francis, Press Conference, Vatican, 18th March 2013.

[13] Pope Francis with Antonio Spadaro, *My Door is Always Open, A Conversation on Faith, Hope and the Church in a Time of Change*, Bloomsbury, 2014, p. 18.

[14] Pope Francis, *Misericordiae Vultus, Bull of Indiction of the Extraordinary Jubilee of Mercy*, §3.

[15] Pope Francis, *Audience to the Plenary session of the Pontifical Council for the New Evangelisation*, 29th May 2015.

72

[16] *Pope Francis, Conversations with Jorge Bergoglio, The Authorised Biography*, Sergio Rubin and Francesca Ambrogetti, Hodder & Stoughton, 2013, pp. 33-34. Pope Francis with Antonio Spadaro, *My Door is Always Open, A conversation on Faith, Hope and the Church in a Time of Change*, Bloomsbury, 2014, pp. 32 and 33.

[17] Pope Francis with Antonio Spadaro, *My Door is Always Open, A conversation on Faith, Hope and the Church in a Time of Change*, Bloomsbury, 2014, p. 34.

[18] Jorge Bergoglio, *presentation of the book by Luigi Giussani L'attrattiva Gesù*, 27th April 2001. See also Chapter 8 of Robert Moynihan Pray for Me - the life and spiritual vision of Pope Francis, Riderbooks, 2013.

[19] *Ibidem.*

[20] Pope Francis, *Audience to the Plenary session of the Pontifical Council for the New Evangelisation*, 29th May 2015.

[21] Pope Francis, *Homily*, Parish Church of St Anne's in the Vatican, 17th March 2013.

[22] Pope Francis, *Angelus*, 17th March 2013.

[23] Pope Francis, *Press conference during the return flight*, 28th July 2013. Kairos is a Greek word which means "favourable time, a time of grace"'

[24] Pope Francis, *Address to the parish priests of the diocese of Rome*, 6th March 2014.

[25] Pope John XIII, *Gaudet mater ecclesia*, Opening Address of the Second Vatican Council, 11th October 1962.

[26] Pope Paul VI, Encyclical Letter *Ecclesiam Suam* 'On the Church', 6th August 1964.

[27] Pope Francis, *Angelus*, 17th November 2013.

[28] Pope Francis, *Angelus*, 15th September 2013.

[29] Pope Francis, *Homily, Mass for the possession of the chair of the bishop of Rome*, 7th April 2013.

[30] Pope Francis, *General Audience*, 27th March 2013.

[31] Pope Francis, *Homily, Mass for the possession of the chair of the bishop of Rome*, 7th April 2013.

[32] Pope Francis, *General Audience*, 27th March 2013.

[33] Pope Francis, *Angelus*, 15th September 2013.

[34] Pope Francis, *Homily, Mass for the possession of the chair of the bishop of Rome*, 7th April 2013.

[35] Pope Francis, *Misericordiae Vultus*, Bull of Indiction of the Extraordinary Jubilee of Mercy, par. 3.

[36] Pope Francis, *Angelus*, 25th August 2013.

[37] Pope Francis, *Daily Meditation*, Thursday 20th March 2014.

[38] Pope Benedict XVI, Encyclical Letter *Deus Caritas Est,* n. 6.

[39] Pope Francis, *Misericordiae Vultus, Bull of Indiction of the Extraordinary Jubilee of Mercy,* §15.

[40] Cf. Pope Francis, Apostolic Exhortation *Evangelii Gaudium*, §20: "A Church which goes out... all of us are called to take part in this new missionary 'going forth' ".

[41] Pope Francis, *Message for the 52nd World Day of Prayer for Vocations*, 26th April 2015.

[42] Pope Francis, *Message for Lent*, 2015.

[43] Pope Benedict XVI, *Homily*, Our Lady of Loreto Square, 4th October 2012.

[44] Pope Francis, *Daily Meditation*, 17th April 2015.

[45] *Ibidem.*

[46] Pope Francis, *Press conference during the return flight*, 28th July 2013.

[47] Pope Francis, *General Audience*, 18th June 2015.

[48] Pope Francis, *Homily*, Mass with the new Cardinals, 15th February 2015.

[49] Pope Francis, *Misericordiae Vultus, Bull of Indiction of the Extraordinary Jubilee of Mercy*, §12.

[50] Pope Francis, *Misericordiae Vultus, Bull of Indiction of the Extraordinary Jubilee of Mercy*, §19, §2.

[51] Pope Francis, *Homily*, Celebration of Penance, 13th March 2015.

[52] Pope Paul VI, Apostolic Constitution *Mirificus Eventus*, On the Extraordinary Jubilee Year, 7th December, 1965 (there is no official translation in English, only Latin and Italian).

[53] Pope Paul VI, Apostolic Constitution *Mirificus Eventus*, On the Extraordinary Jubilee Year, 7th December, 1965.

[54] Pope Francis, *Homily*, Celebration of Penance, 13th March 2015.

[55] Pope Francis, *Daily Meditation*, Monday 2nd March 2015.

[56] Pope Francis, *Daily Meditation*, Tuesday 3rd March 2015.

[57] Pope Francis, *Angelus*, Sunday 8th March 2015.

[58] Pope Francis, *Address to participants in a course on the internal forum organised by the Apostolic Penitentiary*, 12th March 2015.

[59] Pope Francis, *Daily Meditation*, 29th April 2013. There is not a full translation of this homily in English.

[60] *Ibidem.*

[61] Pope Francis, *Daily Meditation*, 23rd January 2015.

[62] Pope Francis, *General Audience*, 19th February 2014.

[63] Pope Francis, *Homily, Mass for the possession of the chair of the bishop of Rome*, 7th April 2013.

[64] Pope Francis, *General Audience*, 19th February 2014.

[65] Pope Francis, *General Audience*, 10th September 2014.

[66] Pope Francis, *Angelus*, 15th September 2013.

[67] Pope Francis, *Homily, Mass for the faithful of the Armenian Rite*, 12th April 2015.

[68] Pope Francis, *Homily, Mass for the possession of the chair of the bishop of Rome*, 7th April 2013.

[69] Cf St Bernard, *Sermon 61, 3-5: Opera Omnia, 2, 150-151*.

[70] Pope Francis, *Homily, Mass for the faithful of the Armenian Rite*, 12th April 2015.

Mercy Works

Mark P. Shea

The spiritual and corporal works of mercy are not a list to be learnt but actions to be lived. Mark Shea gives great examples of people who have performed the works of mercy and advice on how we can practice them in the 21st Century. Pope Francis's Year of Mercy is a call to each one of us to rediscover and to live the works of Mercy every day.

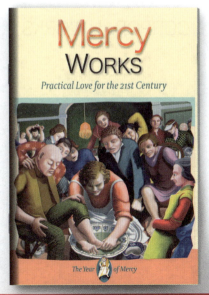

PA25   ISBN 978 1 78469 076 2

Corporal Works of Mercy

Mgr Richard Atherton

Feeding the hungry and thirsty, clothing the naked, housing
the homeless, visiting the imprisoned, the sick, and burying the
dead - Pope Francis wants us to stop and think again, especially
during the Year of Mercy. Are these things I can do, or are they
for others to get on with? What good do they do? Actions of
mercy are often terribly ordinary and doable. Fr Atherton guides
us through the spiritual and practical matters that Love asks of
all Christians.

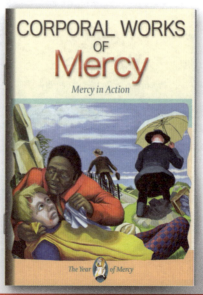

SP45   ISBN   978 1 78469 080 9

Spiritual Works of Mercy

Mgr Paul Grogan

Most Christians want to live an active faith yet feel perplexed about how to do so. The seven interconnected 'spiritual works of mercy' come to our aid: counselling the doubtful; instructing the ignorant; admonishing sinners; comforting the afflicted; forgiving offences; bearing wrongs patiently; and praying for the living and the dead .Through such acts of mercy we can respond fully to God's goodness towards us, involving conversion of our interior life: such acts are truly God's acts of mercy; we, mere human agents for God to alleviate people's unhappiness.

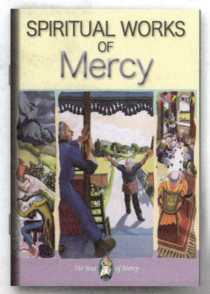

SP46   ISBN 978 1 78469 087 8